Start-Up Connections

TOYS

Stewart Ross

First published in this edition in 2011

Published by Evans Brothers Limited
2A Portman Mansions
Chiltern Street
London W1U 6NR

Produced for Evans Brothers Limited by
White-Thomson Publishing Ltd.,
+44 (0) 843 2087 460
www.wtpub.co.uk

Printed & bound in China by New Era Printing Co. Ltd.

Editor: Anna Lee
Consultant: Nora Granger
Designer: Tessa Barwick

Cover (centre): Noah's Ark.
Cover (top left): Victorian alphabet blocks and modern
    teddy bear.
Cover (top right): clockwork car and Barbie doll.

British Library Cataloguing in Publication Data

Ross, Stewart
  Toys. - (Start-up history)
  1.Toys - History - Juvenile literature
  I.Title
  790.1'33'09

ISBN: 978 0 237 54365 5

Acknowledgements: The publishers would like to
thank Big Kids Toy Shop, Lewes, for their assistance
with this book.

Picture Acknowledgements: Beamish Open Air Museum
(cover, top centre right), 5 *(top)*, 10-11, 13 *(bottom)*; Hodder
Wayland Picture Library 7; Mary Evans Picture Library 11;
Zul Mukhida *(cover, top centre left)*, 4 *(top)*, 6, 12, 14,
20 *(top)*, 21 *(right)*; Robert Opie *(cover, top far left)*, 13 *(top)*,
15 *(right)*; Topham Picturepoint *(cover, top far right)*,
15 *(left)*, 19 *(left)*; Victoria and Albert Museum Picture
Library 4 *(bottom)*, 9 *(top)*, 16, 18, 19 *(right)*, 20 *(bottom)*,
21 *(left)*; Richard Stansfield/York Castle Museum *(cover,
centre)*, 5 *(bottom)*, 8, 9 *(right)*, 17 *(left and right)*.

VISIT OUR WEBSITE
Evans
www.evansbooks.co.uk

Contents

Toys now and then

▼ **This is a new computer game.**

It plays a football game.

► **Your parents may have played with a doll like this.**

It was made 40 years ago.

new computer game plays football

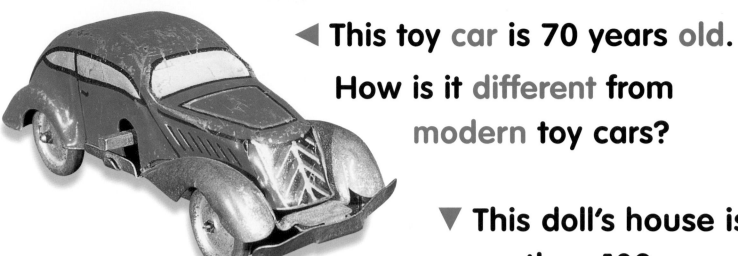

◀ This toy car is 70 years old. How is it different from modern toy cars?

▼ This doll's house is more than 100 years old.

doll   years   ago   car   old   modern   5

What is it made of?

Here is a modern toy dog.
Like most modern toys,
it was made in
a factory.

The dog is
very shiny.
It is made
of plastic.

dog   factory   shiny

These children are playing with a plastic tea set.

Many toys are made of plastic nowadays.
What others can you think of?

plastic   tea set   nowadays   7

Looking at the past

This Noah's Ark was made long ago.

In the past, many toys were made of wood.

They were painted by hand.

Noah's Ark long ago past wood

▼ These old Minibrix are made of rubber.

► This toy soldier is made from lead. How is it different from a modern toy?

painted minibrix rubber soldier lead 9

A Victorian steam engine

► These children are playing with a Victorian steam engine.

Victorian   steam engine

Steam engines have a burner
to heat the water.

The water turns into steam.
The steam drives the engine.

burner   water

Toys to help us learn

▲ Here is a modern computer for children.

It helps them learn to read and do sums.

Meccano build

▼ **Meccano** teaches children how to **build** things. Your grandparents may have played with Meccano.

▲ These alphabet bricks are more than 100 years old.

What did children learn with these bricks?

alphabet bricks 15

Toys from long ago

These toys are from long ago.
Can you see how they work?

◄ This is an old puppet.

◄ Here is a spinning top.

work   puppet

◄ **This toy is called a zoetrope.**

▼ **This card slots into the zoetrope.**

When the zoetrope spins around, the figures move.

How do we know?

► A rag doll.

These dolls were made at different times.

Can you tell which is the oldest and which is the newest?
How can you tell?

oldest   newest

◀ **A plastic doll.**

◀ **A china doll.**

rag   **china**   **19**

The same and different

One toy car is modern and one is 70 years old.
How can you tell which is which?

teddy bears   different

These teddy bears were made at different times.
One is new and one is about 90 years old.

Some modern toys are like toys made long ago.
Other toys have changed over time.

times   changed

Further information for Parents and Teachers

TOYS ACTIVITY PAGE

Use the activities on these pages to help you to make the most of *Toys*.

Activities suggested on this page support progression in learning by consolidating and developing ideas from the book and helping the children to link the new concepts with their own experiences. Making these links is crucial in helping young children to engage with learning and to become lifelong learners.

Ideas on the next page develop essential skills for learning by suggesting ways of making links across the curriculum and in particular to literacy, personal development and ICT.

WORD PANEL

Check that the children know the meaning of each of these words from the book.

• ago	• different	• new/ newest	• rubber
• batteries	• factory	• nowadays	• shiny
• changed	• hand-painted	• old/ oldest	• times
• china	• lead	• past	• Victorian
• clockwork	• long ago	• plastic	• work
• computer game	• modern	• radio-controlled	

MAKING A CLASS ONLINE TOY MUSEUM

1) Select your toys
Discuss what kinds of toys you plan to have in your museum.

- Modern toys, to make a collection for future generations to look back on, to toys from more than one generation.
- Toys aimed at a particular age of child, or those aimed at a variety of ages.
- Toys from a particular culture, or those from many cultures.
- Toys which are in good condition or those which have been used and show signs of wear.
- A particular kind of toy, e.g. soft toys or moving toys, or toys in general.

2) Select a model for your online collection
Together browse the internet looking for online collections of toys or online toy museums. For example, look at:

- toy collections in the world's big online museums e.g. www.vam.ac.uk
- specialist collections e.g. www.ltmcollection.org/museum/index.html
- individual blogs e.g. http://www.btinternet.com/~valandgreig.chisholm/collectables/
- sites for collectors e.g. www.ebay.co.uk

Decide which of these sites you want to model your online toy museum on.

3) Decide what kind of information you want to present
You need to make some joint presentation decisions, for example:

- Will you include video or digital photos?
- Can each person write what they want to, or will you create a form for everyone to complete about their toy?

You will also need to decide how to organise the toys in your collection. You could, for example, organise by:

- age of toy
- material
- age, gender or culture of child intended to play with the toy
- purpose of the toy e.g. fun, learning, building, board games, TV tie-ins etc.

4) Create your online toy museum
You should be able to create your online toy museum as a class blog either on your website or on your VLE. Your school ICT co-ordinator will be able to make a recommendation.

- Draw up a visual plan, so that everyone knows what the agreed organisation will be.
- Organise a neutral background against which children can take photographs or make videos of their toys.
- Support children in creating their text.
- Share the url with the wider community, and invite members of the community to come and talk to your class about their old toys.

USING TOYS FOR CROSS-CURRICULAR WORK.

As citizens in 21st-century Britain, it is important that children develop key competencies as

- successful learners
- confident individuals and
- responsible citizens.

Cross-curricular work is particularly beneficial in developing the thinking and learning skills that contribute to building these competencies because it encourages children to make links, to transfer learning skills and to apply knowledge from one context to another. As importantly, cross-curricular work can help children to understand how schoolwork links to their daily lives. For many children, this is a key motivation in becoming a learner.

The web below indicates some areas for cross-curricular study. Others may well come from your own class's engagement with the ideas in the book.

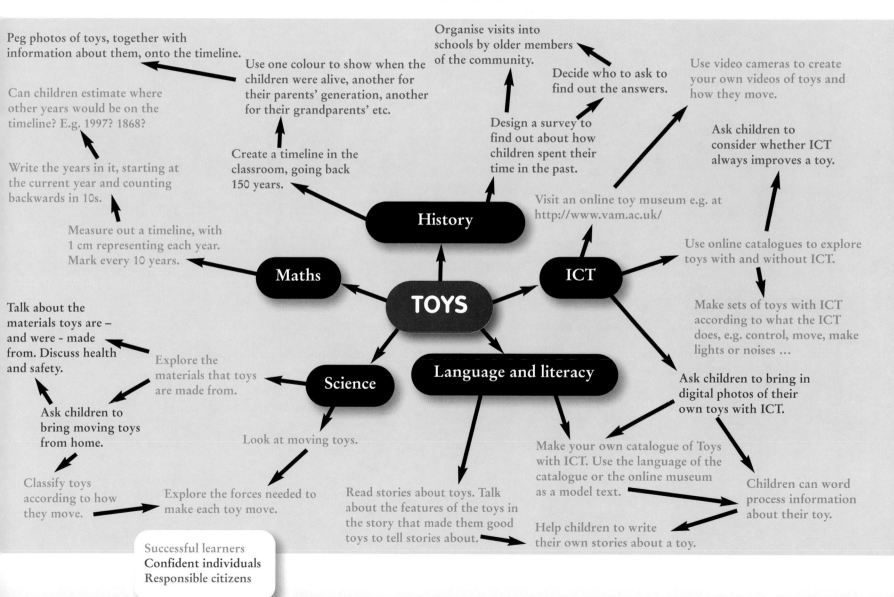

Peg photos of toys, together with information about them, onto the timeline.

Can children estimate where other years would be on the timeline? E.g. 1997? 1868?

Write the years in it, starting at the current year and counting backwards in 10s.

Measure out a timeline, with 1 cm representing each year. Mark every 10 years.

Use one colour to show when the children were alive, another for their parents' generation, another for their grandparents' etc.

Create a timeline in the classroom, going back 150 years.

Organise visits into schools by older members of the community.

Decide who to ask to find out the answers.

Design a survey to find out about how children spent their time in the past.

Use video cameras to create your own videos of toys and how they move.

Ask children to consider whether ICT always improves a toy.

Visit an online toy museum e.g. at http://www.vam.ac.uk/

Use online catalogues to explore toys with and without ICT.

Make sets of toys with ICT according to what the ICT does, e.g. control, move, make lights or noises …

History

Maths

ICT

TOYS

Talk about the materials toys are – and were - made from. Discuss health and safety.

Explore the materials that toys are made from.

Ask children to bring moving toys from home.

Science

Language and literacy

Look at moving toys.

Classify toys according to how they move.

Explore the forces needed to make each toy move.

Read stories about toys. Talk about the features of the toys in the story that made them good toys to tell stories about.

Make your own catalogue of Toys with ICT. Use the language of the catalogue or the online museum as a model text.

Help children to write their own stories about a toy.

Ask children to bring in digital photos of their own toys with ICT.

Children can word process information about their toy.

Successful learners
Confident individuals
Responsible citizens

23

Index